Birth
& What Came After

poems on motherhood
by Jessica Bates

Contents

/art/

To the doulas, the midwives,
the mothers, the sisters.
To the women who birth us all.

Birth & What Came After

Well,

_____

I almost didn't use my own topless
body for the cover but
I'm my own muse
and I hope you're yours too.

And for those who have a problem
as Thumper would say
(and so would my mom):
If you don't have something nice to say
then don't say anything at all.

_____

As a young child I'd tell you
I wanted six kids.

When I hit puberty, motherhood
didn't seem so glamorous anymore.
I couldn't stand the idea of sticky hands
roaming over me, answering only to the name:
Mom.
Yuck. Eye roll.

And so, for many years I resisted. Maybe
I'll have no children. Maybe
I'll only adopt. And then
I started to wonder about my own belly
stretching, about my own cells
mixing with my husband's and
spitting out something new, something
uniquely us, him and me.

And I rolled that beneath my tongue
and I tested it in my head. And I looked
at my hands and imagined a baby in them.
And even though I couldn't picture it,
not at all, I decided to do it
to throw out the birth control
to let nature play its course.

Fetus

___

Every tummy ripple gets attention now.
Is that baby, or gas?
No sickness, only tender breasts.
Just a little tired.

The cat is clawing its slow way
out of the bag.
Soon it will be evident, the secret
will pop from beneath my skin,
people will reach out to touch it,
to bless it,
to receive a blessing.

Some goo on my belly,
a white sheet.
A room of held breath.
We saw the little thing squirm,
so much movement, the tadpole
tiny in the giant ocean of me.
We saw the heart pumping, glug-glug,
through the chest.
We saw blood pulse in and out of the
umbilical cord,
the liver, the brain,
like colors alive on a heat map.
The bones looked long.
The ultrasound tech measured them,
click-click.
We waited, trailing down the
tiny skeleton body,
stopped and held between the legs.

It's a boy, she told us.

He turned toward us, hands in prayer.
We saw the deep black of
his eye sockets.
We watched his profile as
he sucked a thumb.
He turned away from us,

slung an arm over his head.

My mother was quiet
until we got to the parking garage.
There she let loose a cry.
A grandson.

After the ultrasound
I went to hear Peter Heller read
from his new book *The Painter*.
I loved his book *The Dog Stars*.
I sat in the audience like I had a secret. And
I did.
A son wrapped within me,
a warm tight cocoon.
After the reading, he took questions.
I asked whether he was
a fast or slow writer.
His answer was winding &
lovely & detailed,
but all I remember now was:
Fast.
And he smiled a real smile
when I told him
I had a son on the way.
He wished me luck.
He has a warm smile.

Gary Shteyngart said, *Nanny up*,
when I asked him nine months pregnant and
drenched with rain
how he was able to balance
parenthood & writing.

                              I frowned.
                    I couldn't afford a Nanny.

f   a   s   t   /   f   o   r   w   a   r   d

Two years later, Zadie Smith came
to town & of course I went.
When asked (by someone else) about
motherhood & writing, she gave
an honest answer.
She wasn't able to write at home
with her kids home. They were always
coming in, asking things.
Already, I got this. But she didn't
put it down, mothering & writing.
She was just real with it. You can do it,
just get out of the house.
While she signed her name in my
copy of *Swing Time* I thanked her
for the practical advice.

Birth requires stamina, strength.
A midwife told me walking was
great training for birth,
and so I walked.

I made a birthing playlist
and I held my phone
in my hands and I played music.
I walked and walked.
Our backyard is compact so I did laps.

Loop this tree, loop that tree
and back again.
I watched the trees wave their branches,
saw the birds fly away.
I watched the moon rise.

I walked. I walked so much
that my feet made a path
through the grass.
My dogs followed me at first. Soon
they became bored with the laps,
then they watched me.

Sometimes I imagined
birthing my son.
Sometimes I walked blankly.

Sometimes I walked in fear
and other times
I walked in confidence.
Every day, I walked.

I was present at my birth,
though I don't remember it.
My mother's water broke weeks early,
my feet were down,
and the doctor cut me out.
Staples in her stomach grew infection.
My mom was sick.

I was present at the birth
of my first sister.
As my mother labored I walked the halls
of the hospital with my aunt.
It took forever.
I remember being tired. I wanted to meet
her but I fell asleep
for the action. I only recall
the pale green hospital gown
the staff let me keep.
It lived in a box of dress-up clothes.

I was present at the birth
of my second sister.
We skipped school to be in the room.
I stood close, my aunt and I,
right beside the doctor.
I saw the whole thing, legs open, head
peeking through the gap,

slowly, slowly, and then —
Whoosh! Here comes the body!
Sweet release.

I was present for the birth of my niece.
I dropped my nephew off
at daycare, drove
through Florida streets
to the hospital, met my
sister-in-law just in time for the epidural. I
wound her thick hair into
a bun high on her head. Her husband
watched from a laptop in Afghanistan,
drinking a fake beer.
I held one leg back,
her friend held the other,
PUSH PUSH PUSH.
My niece came quickly,
her mother was strong.
She made it look easy.

I've read a hundred birth stories
and still I cannot picture myself
opening. Splitting.
giving life.

These are the things no one talks about. There was pregnancy. Things happen to your body, but the birth looms in the distance and like a strong dark wall there is nothing past it. You cannot see past it.

The body forgets pain, she said. Otherwise women would only have one child. Is it true? Has my body forgotten?

It has been almost five months, and here is what I remember: I felt the urge to pee a thousand times, but I could never go. I sat on the toilet of the hospital bathroom and tried to push a body out. I tried to just sit easily and let the body slip out. I tried to sneeze and feel it shoot out. I existed as many separate pieces: a voice in my head, a naked heaving belly draped occasionally with a white hospital sheet, a woman, surrounded by friends and family as she sweated and breathed through rushes of energy bumping through the body. I existed in my doula's hands that rubbed and kneaded and caressed me for an entire rotation of the earth. And in other ways I existed nowhere during these hours, they are a different life.

It makes no sense to write about it chronologically now. My mother threw a blanket over the wall clock. The time, the time. In one hour I'll have my baby. In one more hour. It was a trap, a maze. My grandpa was obsessed with clocks. What is time even for?

At 10 am I travelled into my body and found my sack of water and told it, break!, and it listened. I was a glistening goddess, naked and pacing. My mother brushed and braided my hair. I breathed forever, just breathed. In out. In out. It will not, cannot, last forever.

We were all suspended in a white cloud that knew no minute hand. There was just me, a heavy body that cracked ever so slowly open. And then I split in two and he was born, blue and quiet. I felt raw and inside out. I felt the power of my body, and I felt no pain.

Song for my First Sister

My sister puts her head on my shoulder
while I breastfeed my son.
She rubs his head with her hand.
His head so like mine.
Her hand so like mine.
Our heads together, hair mixing.
My sister speaks in actions.

My sister who organized baby clothes when
small tasks overwhelmed me.
My sister who stayed with me through hours of
labor,
while the sun set, rose, and set again.
My sister who cut the chord
separating my son from me
ushering him from one plane to another,
inside to out.

I hardly remember life before she
was my sidekick.
Her in the store with a baby doll,
me with a book, us both hurrying to catch
our speed-walking
grocery-shopping mother.

Later, us in the car singing to the radio
on our way to high school.

Me asking her to read
procrastinated homework
aloud to me on our drive to school.
Her complaining, then relenting.
reading for me and fighting car-sickness.

My sister the tender-heart but not
tender-hearted.
Warrior sister,
smart and succinct sister,
never using too many words.

My sister who holds my son's body
while his head bobs on my breast, feeding.
Thoughts alien to me spill in her brain,
but still the same hair mixes,
such twin heads rest on each other,
such kindred smiles shine
from our faces.
We are so different.
We are not so different.

Two random expressions of our parents
and their parents before them.
Two sisters growing into mothers.
Time slipping slowly, steadily into the
unknown, into the sparkly future.

Song for my Second Sister

Freckled sister, funny sister,
I stood breathless behind the doctor while mom
pushed you out.

I skipped school that day, and so did
our other sister.
We waited waited waited waited
and then you were there.
Hello, sister. Welcome.
I was nine.

I don't remember much about
our mother that day,
but I remember the energy in the room
like water ready to break down a wall.

Two perfect decades later you nap while I labor,
you laugh and talk with our sister while
I labor,
you snack. You go to class and you
come back. Still, I'm in labor.

You skipped your evening class,
good thing!,
because that's when he
pushed his way out.

I remember your face scrunched
in disgust.

You stood gripping hands with
our sister, eyes on my spread legs.
I wanted to give birth squatting
but instead I was lying on a bed,
wringing my body with each contraction, and
between them pretending I was dead.

(There's a buddhist meditation
where you lie still,
you play dead, you see your skin
rot and fall away,
your muscles dissolve,
your bones turn to ash
and the wind wipes you away.)

I remember your face calm
and free of worry.
You sister, used to want to cut
people open and inspect them
after death.

The midwife called, move the light!,
and you jumped to help
before any of the nurses,
little assistant midwife sister.

When he slipped from me,
finally
finally
blue and wet and warm, hello world!,
I remember your face wide open in awe.

Love Song for my Baby Boy

He's sixteen days new.
I sit with leaky nipples and a beer.
I did not cry until today.

After birth I feel lower down to
the ground.
I feel grounded.
I feel plugged in.

The way he moves when
he's startled —
hands fly out,
a cliff jump.

How far can those
wide eyes see?
How strange that
he came from us
but he is not us.

How strange that
we'll never be as
physically close
as when he was
wrapped beneath my skin.

Life and death both so close
but really
I'm invincible baby.
I blow with the wind.
I rise with the moon.
I bloom with the sunflower.
I rage with the flame.

After birth, the best and
most terrible trip I've ever taken,
I know my strengths and my worsts.
I have seen the other side.
We are no better than the tiger,
the elephant, the beetle, the bee.
Maybe we are worse.
We are the animals, humans,
who spend so much time
denying we're animals.
We spend so much time
talking in circles.
What's the point?
We communicate now,
my son and I
with grunts and pants
and eyes and mouths.

Birth happens all sorts of ways,

as do deaths. The coming in
and the going out,
the entrances and exits.

You are so small
and there are so many ways
you could die.

I dreamed I dropped you
from the top of a steep staircase.
I watched your body bounce down.

My hand on your head is like
palming a fuzzy peach.
I could crush you.
Zipping up your sleep sack
reminds me so much of
a body bag.

I am lucky enough to have a village. I have a mother who doesn't wait for me to ask for help. In the days after the birth, my first, she filled our fridge with food, she held my son and told me to go soak in a bath. I was high from the birth, soaring when I looked at him, but I was confused when I looked at me. Who was I? I was learning to feed him from my body, I was learning this new body, the breasts full and arms aching. I was learning that my husband and I weren't ever going to be the same. We had bonded ourselves together in a way that a marriage certificate never would.

My body had been cracked in half. I moved so slowly around the house, up the stairs and out of chairs especially. I had been through something hard and I hadn't processed it yet. A few days later I went up the stairs at a normal human pace and I cheered, my sister cheered with me.

Even with a village, the best village, it was hard. But it had a rhythm, a cozy one. Deep like a drum.

The rhythm was feed, feed, feed, rest.

The first thirty days were a haze of round the clock feedings and diaper changes. They were a fog of kisses and warm quick naps and staring at the beautiful alien body that came out of me. There was crying and frustration and red-rimmed eyes. The whole house sagged without sleep.

I was learning him, this wild thing that came from me. Even though I loved him from the first moment, I didn't recognize him. I had to study his knuckles, the curve of the bones in his hand. I watched the lips at my nipple, and I watched the cheeks pumping like a beating heart. I slept when I could. Sometimes though, instead of sleeping, I just held him. Watched him. Felt the tiny skeleton, the pebble bones of his spine. I blinked in the milky hours before daylight, watching his pulse blink in his forehead.

I watched my husband hold him. I discovered new things to love, new challenges and strains and inspirations that weren't there before. It is work to grow in the same direction. We find moments to connect again, ways to remember how we were before. We hold each other up.

All this information writes over old memories, and in some ways there's a time wall there, at the birth. I can remember things from before but they are cut off; I will never return. I am so much stronger than I ever knew, and my wellspring of love runs deep. It's connected down at the root to a deep eternal love, and there's a flowing river there I can always drink from.

I will never be the same. And that's great.

First published in Mama, Bare, *a collection of new mother stories curated by Kristen Hedges.*

1
I thought it would be easy, said a
new mom at the baby shower.
Baby. Boob.
What more is there?, she said.

But it is easy for us, little one,
and it has been since the beginning.
I've always known these breasts
were perfect,
I just misunderstood
their divine purpose.
They are not for enticing men
into buying me drinks
on a dark dance floor. They are not
for showing off on a poolside
Miami afternoon.
These perfect nipples are,
have always been,
for you.

Your wide wet eyes were open
from the start,
shining black with the density
of a universe.
Your mouth open and hungry,
your head rolling like a drunk.

You were perfect at it, too, the sucking.
The sustenance.

We feed everywhere, when and
wherever you tell me you're hungry.
I did not know how much I'd like it.
This is something no one talked about,
or not much anyway, not in a way
I could grasp.

I duck my arm out of clothing
and free my breast.
You swivel your head toward me,
tongue thrusting.
This is a dance that we've perfected,
the feeding.
Twin lines of electricity run through me,
up and down, head to toe.

2
O, drink from me, sweet son
who came from the black depths
of my body.
You latch on and power up,
drawing energy from my currents.
I shoot you little shards
of bone and with them your body
continues its work, building the bone, brewing
the blood, fattening
the folds of you.
You suck and I tingle from skull to heel,

struck with a tuning fork and humming
in the blue light of a darkened bedroom.

I try to feel my own edges in the
low light. I send my mind to the
outer edges of me — where do I end?
I send myself to my innermost edges,
and I see that in both directions
I am infinite.

Everything is soft, every part of you and
every part of me. I hold you long after you've
come unlatched.
Your sleeping mouth sucks
a phantom teat, your fingers clutch
my thumb and turn white.
That perfect invisible boob has you
sleep smiling, sending you off into a dream, into
dreamland,
la la, the whimsical dust of sleep whisking you
away
somewhere I cannot follow.

I shuck the husk of you into bed,
feet twitching and eyes rolling, lips
open and circling into ecstasy.

These are the days you sleep on me,
across my tummy with a milky face.
These are the days I sip coffee cold
or lukewarm or a thousand
temperatures in between.

These are the days of doing
nothing except
watching your face, learning you.
You prop a loose fist on your cheek.
your eyelids streak with
purple lightning,
blood pulses through the dome
of your closed eye.
Your sleeping eye dreams of things
I'll never know.

These are the days of productivity
meaning:
> Eating three meals.
> Showering.
> Running laundry, maybe folding.
> Bathing baby.
> Having sex.

These are the days of your babyhood,
the days of diapers and giggles and

sucking on fingers. The days we
are cozy in our castle, rain pinging
off windows, toes cold and alive,
sweatshirts and blankets
draped over every surface.

These days will not last.
I drink them, thirsty for more.

Goddess pose up and down the hallway,
my son dangling like a leaf
from my fingers.
Muddy Waters on two worn
warm speakers while two
of my favorite humans paint —
oil on canvas,
then, later, oil on the growing mural.

> *The gypsy woman told my mother*
> *before I was born*
> *You got a boy child comin'*
> *Gonna be a son of a gun*

I feel the music way back in my bones.
My son feels the rhythm,
it moves him, too.

I see them painting and want to
make a fresh stroke on a canvas
and get lost. I feel jealous that he needs me,
then that feeling gone
like smoke and I smile at my son
cutting his first two fresh white teeth.
I smile at this boy who will be
a masterpiece. Who by existing is
a masterpiece. His fingers grip mine

as he squeals up and down,
up and down the hall.

Paint party night used to mean
art with friends, wine flowing and music waving
through us and colors scratched and yawned
onto canvas.
Now it meant something different:
I was keeping the son happy and walking and
occupied.

Paint party is over for today.
It doesn't matter. Because now even though the
boy is sick and teething and hot and oozing
green snot, I leave the room and I go downstairs
and put on headphones and put on music and
pretend I am someone else,
pretend I am me.
It takes me a while to shed the guilt and wiggle
out, to loosen the jaw of attachment, to let

go.

It takes me too many words to say what I mean.

— for subby & mote

Surely in the wild they gave babies
bones to gnaw on.

It is painful to grow teeth.
His gums are red, raw, stretched
to bursting. His face hot.

Fresh rows of bone glint through the
gum, and I think of sprouts
peeking through the tender earth.

I see why it's called *cutting teeth*.
The teeth slice into my nipple like razors
and I yelp and growl. *No.* I say.
Don't bite me. He hears, and
he doesn't again.

I never knew teeth took so long to grow,
but every few months we're here again,
the drooling, the biting on fingers, the
dull persistent pain, the hot hot face —
and I wish, again and again,
I could cut them instead.

Koshi Mama Black as Night

Every time it gets hard, really hard,
I just realize that I have to give more,
love more, open more.
There is always more in me,
I keep finding it.

Our velvet black dog, invisible
in the night and most of the day,
is a mama herself.
We adopted her in the spring
on a cool day when my son was just
a blip inside me. She came from Alabama, was
adopted, bred, and sent back to the shelter.
Shelter, a place
that keeps you safe
from the elements.

Her nipples are black and long,
and I like to think of five little balls of fur
tugging at her.
I'm sure she was happy then.
Is she happy now?

On this night, a night when I had
dug deep and wasn't sure
I had anything left,
my sweet velvet black girl came to me.

My face was wet with tears
and my breath heaved.

She licked me, my hands, my face.
She leaned her body against me,
invited me to lean my weight
against her,
and I did.

Outside of our home I built a force field.
Every night I bless it and it grows.

Outside of the winter ground the trees shed their
skin.
The sun is white and not yellow.

Outside of my body, an extension of me, my son
breathes.
Outside of me he yawns and bleats,
pecks at me when he's hungry or bored.

Outside our walls our gray wolf dog sits
under the emptiness of a new moon.

Outside of the shower a friendly ghost passes,
tap tapping copper pans on an
upward staircase.

Outside of my heart you'll find the ribs,
outside the gums, the teeth,
outside the head, hair.

Outside of this hemisphere it is summer,
the earth tilted on its side.

Outside of my head there is nothingness.
Inside, black holes rip the stars apart.

Outside our fortress feet slap the
faded winter street.
A guard dog peeks from the slit of a
black curtain.

Outside of the shower my skin stings,
rubbed raw with used coffee grounds.

Outside my periphery my son watches the
pretty ghost dance.

Outside of my force field the rest of the universe
shivers,
a heat dream foaming from my brain.

Your cries are knives going through me.
I am undone.

You are inconsolable. Your dad
sings to you gently, gently. He stays
calm, positive, smiling. I cry and fall
in love with him again and again.

You're finally asleep, and together
your dad and I silently put clean sheets
on the bed in the dark, like a game
kids might play.

Don't wake the baby, shhh.

I pray to the goddess for just a few
hours of easy sleep.

Our home in winter
dark and chilly
like a cave.
I let the dog in
and his fur shines golden blue
in the fading light.
Door shuts and lights lower,
everything tints gray and
my other senses turn on,
fingers feel gently
for the second light switch.
Baby naked upstairs
kicking and singing on a rectangle of
curving cotton.
Dogs playing war nearby,
grunts providing a drum line to
baby's staccato song
like exclamation points
on this perfect day.
Still daylight after 5 pm,
we are shedding our sleepy skin
in the promise of spring.

We look at each other
in the blue night light.
He tears at his own face,
his hind claw hooks
into my ribs, and I fight him
with softness. His dad says,
He has both our fire.
He's too strong.

I hold the animal tight to my chest.
Domestication takes time.
The boy grips a lock
of my hair. *He is stronger*
than both of us, I say. *Gotta break him,*
gotta break him with love.

When life feels heavy,
suffocating,
forget you are a person.

Sit somewhere new — a park bench,
on a flat rock near water, or deep
at the trunk of a tree.

Sit on a busy street and
forget you are a person.

Listen.
Breathe.

I bet if you listen
you can hear it all,
all that has ever been
and all that will come.

Kitchen Window Time Machine

Water falls over my hands
and I scrub the sweet potato like a lover
working out kinks and removing dirt.
Grooming is an act of love.

I see my grandmother at her
kitchen window.
I open blinds and let in light,
that heating kind of light,
and I feel the new energy in the room.

Upstairs, finally, the child sleeps,
the husband is gone, and I
am deliciously alone.

I breathe at my own pace, a slow one.
Oh, that magic feeling, nowhere to go.

Potatoes rubbed with oil, kissed, and buried
deep in the oven's belly to cook.
Then to the remembering, the thinking,
the doing whateverthafuck I want,
the flirtation of the feather-like before.
The blowing in the unpredictable wind.

From the window I see a tree,
a leyland cypress,

thicker on one side, and I stare at its
cluster of branches reaching
to the arc the sun makes
across our domed sky.

How will I explain it to him?
The fact that
we live on a big ball
swinging fast through something
we don't really understand — space! —
and we're beating like hearts,
blipping through time,
teased with crossed wires and
empty promises.

I think of my grandmother, a smell
sweeps over me:
cut grass, warm weighted air
and sunshine, new leaves,
yellow tinged memories,
a warm orange hug from the past and future.

For the first time in more days
than I can count
I drive away from my son,
and I feel myself tugged apart.
The car windshield is too big, too open.
The sky is thin, an invisible gray.
I wonder if any of this is real.

A panoramic sky weeps
easy tears on my window.
Tight jaw. Loud music.
In the front sloping yard of a church
teens plant trees in the rain.
The trees are too close together.
I picture roots tangled.
As above, so below.

He's going longer and longer
without needing me for food.
My body aches for the weight of him,
for the warm heat of his body.
Without him I am so light that
I might float up and away.

I need to leave my son more, I realize,
panicked by the thought of dying,

of leaving him
motherless.
It could happen quick — a semi could smack into
my side,
car crinkled like a beer chugged from both ends.
It's too raw, too selfish,
to go out alone.

These are the thoughts of a
deranged person,
a new mother.
I fold them up in little pieces and
fling them to the wind.

I follow old roads that house memories.
I make it to the store and back home, whole.

I put your fingers to my lips.
Little buds, I kiss them.
I inhale the horrors that have you twitching
fidgeting
and one by one
I suck them in and blow them away.
I hiss at them
and they wince.
I don't know how long they'll stay away
without me watching over you.

I pin you like a bug
to the sheets,
hands make horseshoes over
your thrashing rope arms.
You are warm, a fire licks within you
and it takes all my water,
every molecule of every cell
to simmer you down.

I put my mind with other cool things,
rocks and pebbles and water
rolling over them.

I remember ice on my neck,
water dripping down.

I spread my feet wide on the floor.
I focus on calming myself
completely.
I am nothing but breath.

Finally you loosen,
hands slack,
and with the sweetest sigh
you sleep.

We dressed you in a pale blue collared shirt and navy pants, striped blue socks, all handed down from your cousins and my cousins' children. We rolled the pant legs up to fit you, and still we giggled at how you looked in clothes made for such occasions. You didn't have any shoes. You couldn't walk anyway.

We took you to your first funeral. You pulled one sock off on the way to the church. Old women touched your hand and rubbed your head and asked how old you were. Connie from Atlanta courted you or you courted her and I was the third wheel. It was somber, but it was almost a party. It rode the line.

The visitation was busy, and we shuffled through people and flower displays as big as people. Flowers that die. Still, they are lovely. Still, it's good to be reminded that things die. To enjoy them while they're here. Impermanence. The Buddha.

You could tell the deceased was well-liked because of all the flowers and the sizes of them. You got hungry and I wanted some space, too, so I asked where I could feed you in private. A woman with bangs in a perfect V-shape on her forehead led us to a perfectly preserved dining room.

I sat with my back against a big window, and it was bright out, and there was snow on the ground from a late unwanted storm. We were all needing spring, sunshine, the big battery in the sky. We were all low on fuel. I fed you and we cuddled, and an old gray and white haired woman, a city tour guide, told me her favorite places to take visitors — the Hermitage and Belle Meade Plantation. With you on my breast I cringed inwardly at the word *plantation*, at the way it has always made me feel.

During the funeral service you cooed and gabbed until I had to take you out of the echoing sanctuary. We went downstairs and I changed your diaper on the platform of a podium, and then I held you in an old fancy arm chair and you bit and bit my chin, roaring into me. Some unknowable feeling made you rage, possibly the brevity of life, the absurdity of it all.

In the hallway I listened to the funeral service of a woman I'd never met. A woman who died in a nursing home, heart attack, when days before she was celebrating her great grandson's second birthday.

This woman had left notes and detailed funeral

instructions so her family didn't have to plan a thing. Would I ever be so thoughtful? When they carried her from the church, the pallbearers guided her down the aisle, and I stood holding you far at the edge halfway down a flight of stairs. It was the very same way the bride and groom exit, first, down the aisle, and their guests watch them go, wave goodbye. It may have looked like we were standing in a dugout hole, a grave perhaps, heads poking above ground.

The woman with the V-shaped bangs guided out the grieving, the family sad and busy with all the motions of funeral obligations. I wondered about the woman with the hair, the funeral home worker. Was this a family business? Had she chosen a career filled with death? I could see, almost, the comfort in it. We all end up here. It could be a warm embrace.

The next day we dropped you off with your grandparents, and we went on to the burial. You'll always need a good black suit.

A hole to be filled. A casket lowered into the ground. The casket was closed, and I wondered if the woman had on shoes. I'd like to be buried without them. Just strip off my clothes and curl me into the dirt.

We saw the grave of a baby boy, stillborn. Unnamed. Can you mourn something that doesn't have a name? What do you whisper in the darkness?

My husband put a white flower on the grave. I want to say it was a rose, but I've never cared for plucked flowers so I didn't take notice. Instead I listened to a man behind me sing a hymn. The tune was wobbly and vulnerable, and we all felt the heart, the gravity, the dirt below our feet we were all going back to. A few people joined in. I knew the chorus, but I did not sing. My voice would be far away; it might not even be mine. Eight black hawks flew overhead in a salute or in a military drill, and we marveled at the power we can wield in this short short time, enough power to lift us up and off the earth.

I offered several times
to feed new babies,
to help mothers. It can be
so tiring. Plus I had enough milk
to share.

But each time I offered
I was met with laughter.

She must be joking, they thought.

I wasn't.

The Heart, A Muscle

1

At the heart lives a chakra.
Green, the color we see
the most shades of.
In Tennessee, spring is green
everywhere, fresh new sprout green,
sun-soaked yellow-green
in every pollen-tinted pixel.
See a green hazed valley and us in the center
smiling, skin a-prick and eyes watering.

The heart, the breast, the place
I make milk.
The place I must keep opening, wider,
to make room
for more, prying and widening
until my chest takes up
the whole room then the whole house
and then all of everything.

My heart has surely grown
four sizes or more
and my shoulders are throbbing
from lifting the bulk of him, and I break
open for him and tip back.
I did not know I was a bud, heart
small as a speck and

tight in a ball.
Now the heart is dense, blooming,
flowing and hot.

My heart, like any muscle,
tears apart
and in the in-between spaces it repairs itself,
grows. I feel it thick
inside me, a tender organ, pumping with
newness.

2
A door closes.
A fan pumps cool air onto my fingers.

The midwife tells me:
All hearts in women
who are pregnant
grow about ten percent.
More blood sent to the baby.
After birth, it goes back to normal. Sometimes
there's a murmur.

She listens, silver circle to my heart space.

Yep, I hear it, a little hiccup.
You've given birth.

I didn't know I would miss it,
the blood. The thick yoke, the unbaby,
the familiar low belly ache,
the dark spots in the underwear.

Each month I wonder,
Will it come? And it doesn't,
hasn't, but I still feel the rhythm,
the phantom blood, the moon dance.

And then, the blood comes
like it never left.
I feel the familiar pang
like the smooth scrape on the inside
of the pumpkin before he becomes
the jack-o-lantern.
I smell the familiar scent of shedding,
the mark of fertility.

I look down at the thickness,
red-brown-black and swirling in
toilet water.
It means something different now,
the blood.
It means one that couldn't be.

You're outside me now
but still I shelter you.
You sleep heart against my heart.
I am your earth,
you eat from my breast.
I am the river that nourishes you.
Soon we start to dance, you, the seed
springing forth. You, thick force
at the center.
I am the petals being sucked
sweetly to the sun and away.
You are so fresh and new
and I grow wrinkly. All is well.
I will live forever somewhere.

Drunk in Florida, after a seafood dinner
our mother, the DD, drives my sisters and I
back to the condo.

They're teasing her. We always tease her.
Three-on-one,
how it's always been.

But this night I'm swimming in alcohol, eyes
burning, thinking of when my son
will be old enough to tease me.
Maybe, I say, *we should leave mom alone.*

The sisters turn on me, sink in teeth.
What made you so soft?
They asked.
Since when do you take up for her?

Instead of answering, all I could do was cry.

She sat coiled, right arm
snaked around left, wound
to breaking. She remembered
the room around her. *Unwind*,
she hissed to herself,
and limbs unfolded.

It will all come in time.

Above electric keys, black and white,
is a painting called "The 8:09."

Men, all, boarding a train and
all but one turned away.
Every shadow a man.
Every man in a hat.
Coats to knees, hands in pockets.

The train comes in from the left,
two wide track lines moving closer
to a point where they'll intersect
later, off canvas.

The painting is by Thelma Daxe,
dated 1965.
My son, named from her kin, with the *e*
dropped, our attempt to save pixels
in this strange new world.

The canvas is dark and deep,
the darkness brings a heavy feeling,
and I wonder why Thelma painted this,
such a masculine scene, sad, and I
wonder if the man turned just slightly toward us
is a man she loved
or hated. Or maybe

he's no one she knew at all. Or maybe
the man is her.

At 8:11 the train slips into the tunnel
and my son climbs to the keyboard
and turns up the volume.

There were things I didn't know before I was a mother. I had heard that time was relative, but since I didn't understand time, I had nothing to relate it to. That's the problem with relativity; it always requires an other.

Now I understand it. I've seen the bitch, time. Sometimes I look down at him, this growing one, and he looks different. He wakes up from naps older, no longer fitting nicely in my lap. I notice new patches of hair, a new tint in the eye, a new laugh like ice clinking in a glass. Here's a freckle that wasn't there yesterday.

Screeches and grabs, fists full of hair. Biceps sore from lifting a growing body, a body feeding from my body. Time moves fast. I see his cells changing, I see him grow right in front of me. I am with him that much, watching, that I notice how he is just a blob, and then he eats and sleeps, and then he turns on. As you grow larger, your consciousness increases. He is a universe expanding, and so am I, and one day we'll both pop like balloons.

It's what they all say; time really does move by fast. Where does the time go? Is it a circle or a line? Is it something else?

I've never been so aware of the preciousness of minutes. One minute. One minute of silence, a baby asleep after an hour of cries. The things I can accomplish in a minute while oatmeal is warming. You wouldn't believe. I list them in my head before I decide: pet Baron, pet Koshi, wash the crockpot, wash the breast pump, go kiss my husband and bring him a handful of chocolate. There are so many things to do and to leave undone.

Sometimes I sit in front of him while he kicks naked on the floor, smiling up at me and gurgling some foreign tongue. He watches his hand in disbelief, mouth open like a baby bird: *I'm doing it*, he must be thinking. *I'm the one controlling this thing.*

I unpack the dishwasher in stages: bottom, silverware, top. By the end of the day I've usually emptied it and filled it again. Sometimes I've also loaded and unloaded a batch of laundry that is crumpled on the bed waiting for the moment I come to give it, too, some love.

Every day now, he is different,
taller, face more mature, eyes serious,
legs lengthening and hair thickening,
a C-shaped curl on his smooth forehead.
Yet he's afraid to be on his own,
he wants to crawl back into me,
warm sleep, bliss, wants to feel his cheek
on my cheek and melt
into me and wear my skin.
He doesn't know yet that he doesn't
need me, that one day he'll push
my kiss away, gallop over to friends,
eyes cutting sharp over to me.
The Mother. The portal that delivered
him to earth — from where?
Other kids are talking, others
don't cling desperate to mothers.
Other kids aren't mine. Mine is his own
and will worship his own holy place,
will kiss animals on the mouth, will
giggle at his father and his two wild dogs
playing and one day soon, new battles,
longer legs, more hair on the body, he
will unzip from me and go.

— *after* The Pulling *by Sharon Olds*

On my hand, between thumb and index,
a mole. Right at the pressure point,
the place my mother used to pinch hard
when I had a migraine.
Did the headache dissolve or
was the pain she created greater?

My son, explorer of my body,
plucks at it, the mole. He inspects
its edges, flicks at it
absentmindedly
with his little finger
while he nurses, while he watches a
movie in my lap, while he cuddles
against me in sleep. My imperfection,
his grounding stone.

When he wakes his hand reaches for it,
the mole, tucked in the V of my thumb
and forefinger. When he's anxious
it calms him, fingering it, playing with
its edges. I wonder
if one day he will rip it off, leaving empty
space beneath.

We left our son for a weekend, traveled
to the mountains for a wedding, my son

stayed behind with my mother.
She said in the night he woke,
clawing at her hand, digging for a mark
that wasn't there. Without his constant
poking, my mole ached.

We stopped for gas at a rural rest stop
and I decided to give my son a quick sip.

I pulled out my breast, he sucked.
An old woman came by to say hello.

I always wanted to nurse my babies,
she said, *but I was too shy.*

Sisters Searching for A Grave

This funeral I left my child at home.
We payed our respects to our mother's
boss, a family friend,
a warm strong spirit.

We were in the same place our
grandmother was buried
eighteen years ago. We wanted to find
her resting place.

We each checked our screens but there
was no map. So we followed our mom's
head-spinning directions:
"Drive around to the left sort of near the
main road, and find the big tree and
she's pretty much right under it."
Or something like that, so we curve
around to the left and see the main road.
And so many trees.

We park and look out at the stones
in warped rows. We repeat the name
we're looking for,
like a mantra or a spell.
We split up and cast ourselves wide
and we read name after name of the
shells of the people that rest beneath us.

Headstones worn and bluish green,
corners smoothed from years of wind
rubbed against them.

It took longer but I couldn't resist doing
the math, discovering how old at death.
We searched in silence and when I
found a relative of ours, of our
grandparents, I shouted to my sisters.
They were tiny on the small hill,
came running.
"Not her, but Uncle Charles!" I yelled
and together we stared at it
and wondered how it would be to die
at eighteen, how our grandfather felt,
his younger brother, left alone.
Alive.

And soon after, resting not too far from
Uncle Charles, there was our
grandmother, Martha Agnes, her grave
peaceful and warm and right beneath
a big sturdy sprawling tree
just like our mother said. Beside her
body, we looked at the spot where our
grandfather would join her, when it
was his time to go.

In my memory the three of us are
holding hands, still and quiet as the
dead, watching the wind
move branches of the trees. In my

memory we are barefoot, but surely we
had on shoes. We think of our
grandmother, her thick laugh,
her curly hair, then her bald head
covered with a wig, her love
of gold shoes.
Ghost memories spill over me —
fingers skimming clean white walls,
shirts on a clothesline,
a long sloping yard with a pond at the
bottom, deer and birds and squirrels.
Marlena possessed by the devil on TV
in the sticky afternoon hours
where we lounged on the couch with
cold sweet tea, *like sands through the
hourglass.*

We come from her daughter's womb.
Inside our grandmother was our
mother's body, and inside our
mother's unborn body
she had half of each of us inside her,
three hidden eggs
that would one day turn to three sisters.

Time is messy that way, we are barely
here and we're also eternal.
The sun has moved,
the gravestones darken,
and we must go.

I light a candle and think of
my father's father.
I imagine scenes similar to my childhood
burning at the edges,
imagined, but true in a dimension somewhere.
True by the power
of my thoughts.

I introduce my son to my
dead grandfather.
Fred.
Meet Dax.

Together they inspect the innards
of lawnmowers, cars.
My son learns of tools, their names and their
purposes.
He learns the art of a perfect
grilled cheese.

My grandpa makes fun of my son's
big ears, gives him Coke
even though I ask him to serve only water, gives
him dollar bills as bribery
for chores, tells him he put his picture
in the garden to scare away birds.

My son finds Playboy magazines from the 70s
stashed on the shelf above the washing machine.
He digs for the right shade from
a plastic jack-o-lantern
full of broken crayons. He plays in doghouses
my grandpa built.
My grandpa hands him a hammer and tells him
to knock stray nails back
into the wood.

I can tell
they are cut
from the same cloth.

Let us find the wounds
in ourselves and in each other
and mend them.
Let's kiss our children, let's
tell them the truth.
Let's listen to their hurts
and take them seriously.
They are valid.
Let's teach our hearts
the power of kindness,
the value in every life.

Can't Sleep / the Weight of Pain

Some nights I am awake
trying to sleep but not
realizing my eyes are wide open,
A/C blowing my airballs dry.

I hallucinate handprints on the ceiling,
a girl's face or a woman's
flashes at my corners.

It is dark completely but I have sensors
other than the eyes.

Sometimes on these pulsing itching
soul-crushing nights, I am sure
that soon I will be swallowed up
and with me other beings that I love.

I can feel it moving toward me,
building, gaining strength and speed
like a storm felt in the blood.

My whole body becomes an ear and
I hear every sound of the universe,
raw, throbbing, flapping with sound.

It is not something I can hear or unhear.
I am just a being cracked open,

open to it all
sucking it in like the empty heart of a
black hole.

If sleep comes like a blanket those nights
I never remember,
I just wake with the knowing
of having been other people,
many others,
of having worn their sorrows,
rolled under the weight of them
and stood up alive.

I thought I didn't like babies much.
I never had one of my own.

I was reading to him,
all day
the same book
over and over
and I wanted to be done.

But today he's staring at the books
alone,
inspecting them
flipping pages forward and back,
moving his head in closer.

He pushes cars with straight fingers,
spins the wheels
with a dropped jaw.

He is a perfect
curious being,
and every moment
for him is an opportunity
to learn something new.

The same
is true of me.

The Ones for Me

Give me the dreamers. The ones
living outside, inside. The ones
feeling the shifts of the earth, watching
the sun setting and rising.

Give me the ones with glowing hearts,
with feet that dance because they want
to and they might as well. The ones
who know that being weird makes you
better, softer, more vulnerable
in the best way.

Give me the artists, the ones who
use their hands and fingers and lungs.
The ones with ink smeared on fingers,
paint on pants, heads dizzy with music.

Give me the ones who build an empire
instead of working in someone else's.
the ones who create and must also
destroy.

Give me the ones that know it's okay
to change their minds. Changing is
growth, and when we stop growing
that's the start of death. If it's not
death then I don't know what is.

Someone asked me recently:
Do you regret having him,
some part of you, just a little?

What monster would I be
to say yes, only sometimes
when I want to finish a task
or read a book in peace,
or go to a store alone with
no rush to return?

But then, I wasn't me fully until I
unfolded
and birthed him.
Life is in the way he grasps my fingers.
The smile he gives me
when I walk in the room
is all the breath I need.

I am a water sign
I like hot water
I like my skin red from the heat.
I imagine that somewhere
way back
my grandmother's grandmother's
grandmother's grandmother
walked from the womb of a hot spring,
steam rising from her fully formed body
like a halo, like an aura,
like a protective shield.

I take my time
unloading the dishwasher.
I relish
how neatly spoon
curves around spoon.
These moments are precious.
I think
of whatever I want.
I think of winter
of the sun low in the sky
of hibernation
of the color of bone.

How to Do Things & Be a Mother

You may no longer finish a task
in one sitting.

Start anyway.

Scatter half-finished things
across your life
like ripped pieces of paper —
trust that somehow
they will find themselves
whole and complete
someday.

Learn to
move
in shorter cycles.
Learn to breathe
in longer ones.

I respond to many names.
Sometimes I am different people.
Sometimes I am the me that howls in
the night.
Sometimes I am the sickening silence.
I wear moonlight in my hair and bare
my teeth.

I stand topless under the stars.
Sometimes I smile glinting knives.
Sometimes I caress leather winged bats.
Sometimes I cry at light jetting through
the foam.
I respond to many names.

It is Easter and the sun is out and it isn't too hot. Blooms hang in trees and bees zoom around them. It's that quick in-between time while trees still hold flowers. We assemble ourselves around tables, the tables covered in pastel pink and blue plastic. My son clings to my body, and I reveal three cars from my bag of tricks. His eyes widen at the wheels, he rolls cars and ignores people. The people gathered are from one branch of my family, my mother's mother's side. My mother's mother has been in the ground for 16 years or more. I was never one to keep track of those things, numbers of the living and the dead. That's my sister's job.

The old men at the round table look like a club meeting for the dying, and as soon as I think that thought I feel shame. My grandpa is there. I think of my other grandpa, my dad's dad, dying alone in a hospital. If it happened to him now I would have the courage to be there, to see the chest rise and fall and be still. I was a different person then. A shallower person, more scared and more selfish. Now I am not afraid of death and I would want to witness his, to show him how I will never forget him. I can't stop looking at them and thinking of death.

One of the dying men walks over with his cane. He wants to talk to my son, but my son is shy. My son pushes his head against my chest anticipating being spoken to by a stranger. The old man touches a silver car, his fingers delicate despite their knobbiness. He moves it in a smooth pattern, jutting here and there. In this old man there's still a young boy, and my eyes water for his youth. I could cry about anything. I can tell by the way he pushes the car that he's an artist. He brought me a maple cutting board on my wedding day, one he made by hand. My husband and I use it for cheese. I need to oil it, I think, adding it to my enormous to-do list of tasks that will never be complete.

If I had an egg I would sit it on its end and watch it stand. Eggs are supposed to stand up on their own on the equinox. Magic. Jesus would enjoy that trick.

I wear a jade necklace, smooth and shaped like a crescent moon. It belonged to my husband's father's mother, and when she died it was given to me. I am not fond of jewelry for jewelry's sake, but I enjoy jewelry with meaning. Jade is supposed to ward off evil. I feel the weight of Grandma Corinne's necklace; my son fingers it and grows quiet. A cousin picks him up and walks to the driveway. He shows my son the trees, the white blooms that won't last, the wheels on the big trucks that belong to my cousins and uncles. I eat fried chicken, mashed potatoes, green beans. I wonder, like every day, what all of this is for, if it's a fluke, an accident, a joke. I chew and swallow. I think of my grandparents, how I am made from parts of them.   Parts of the ones before them.

Someone shouts that the egg hunt is starting. I walk out slowly since my mother and sister are tending to my son. I watch the clouds move. I hear water flow through a fountain. My shoe rubs a blister on my foot, but I like discomfort sometimes.

My son isn't sure how the egg hunt works. He picks eggs from his basket and throws them into the grass. We take pictures and giggle. He points at trucks as they breeze by.

He holds one special egg – magenta, with small raised lines that give it a nice texture. He runs a fingernail along the ripples, widens his eyes. He grips the plastic egg and walks back and forth. We watch him in awe, his youth, his innocence. He started as an egg deep within me, and now he walks on two legs. Magic. Miracle.

One day his fingers will grow knobby, he will start to sag. I pray to the goddesses, the gods, the

eggs, the clouds, the trees. I pray to the wind that he will grow old and die well.

In a warm bath
my breasts ache, heavy.
Full sacks pull downward.
Soon the nipples drip
sweet milk
mixing with bath bubbles.

I did not know you would love it so
that I'd love it so
and now here we are more than
two years later, still nursing.

People are ready for us to stop.
I am one of those people,
and other times I'm not.

It has been a great comfort.
It has been a burden.
It has been an honor.
It has been a sacrifice.

We will find a new way to love
each other, new bonds, new comforts.
You probably won't remember suckling
at the teat.
but I will. I will never forget.

But then I realize it's time, and I point
to a square on a calendar and say, *Here.*
This day, we quit.
When I pick the date, I nurse you to
sleep for a nap,
and I stare at your little body in my
arms, not so little

anymore. I weep onto your body. Will I
know how to comfort you? How to
mother without milk?

For a month we nurse less and less,
gradually, we stay busy at the library
and seeing friends and taking walks and
splashing in mud puddles. I practice
saying, *No. Not right now. Not until
bed.* You practice understanding,
waiting. You practice moving past anger.

On the date that was once far away and
now is here, I am nervous. I know,
though, it is time. It is the date
and I am ready, but still, how? The day
goes on and you ask and I say, *No,
there's no more milk at all, it's gone.*

And you don't nap, just keep eating
more, happily, running around
the house, practically running
down the stairs. You are big. Bigger than
ever. Still, milk is the only way
you've learned to rest, only way
I've learned to rest. Before bed
I take a long shower.
I squeeze down the length of my breast,
udder-like.
I watch for the last time as milk squirts
several tiny lines, haphazard, magic.
I have a superpower, creating food

from the folds of my body. I have used it
well. Maybe
I will use it again for another.

In bed, nighttime, you try to burrow
into my body, crawl beneath the sheets
searching for my breasts,
fling yourself away when I say, *No,
no more milk, we must learn to sleep
without it. There's just no more.*

I feel guilt, because there is more.
It's a choice. I'm making it
for all of us. I'm making it for you. You
will grow once you don't need me
for milk, for sleep. You will learn
how to be you, how to count sheep and
calm the body, you will learn
how to be alone and so will I.

Once your rage subsides and your
breathing slows
I pull you onto me, your body warm,
weight welcome, and I breathe and
breathe. You breathe and breathe.
Then, I can tell you're out, the breath
slowed and peaceful.

With you on my chest I think of
the first time I held you this way,
skin to skin, in the bed of a hospital,
body tiny and skin dewy.

I have never loved you more
than I do now, finally resting,
sleep found without the comfort of my
breast.

Look up at the moon. It is big and round. It is white against blue blue velvet. It is the biggest, most beautiful thing you've ever seen. You can tell it curves out to meet you like a pregnant belly, the shading is supple and alive. It is so big and full you could fall into it.

I feel it tingling my skin, the tiny hairs raise like antennae and blow in the constant waves of the universe. I am being pulled from something to something else, I am buzzing and humming and overrun with frequencies, pulses, nowhere is there stillness and nowhere is there quiet. Except in a vacuum. The sleep chamber that keeps out all signals and leaves you fantastically and frightening alone.

Whenever I start to feel alone, I go outside and search the sky, sometimes even in the day. I look up at that big round moon. Go outside, find it. Drink it in. I bet you'll feel better too.

Writing Prompts for Mothers

Use each prompt as a starting point. You may want to set a timer for 5, 10, or 20 minutes and free write. You may want to record yourself speaking in response to each prompt. Use these ideas to spark your own voice, to tell your own story. Don't stress if you stray from the original prompt. Have fun!

- Write about your pregnancy. The first time you felt your baby move. What did you dream your baby would look like? What did you imagine it would be like to hold your baby in your arms?

- Write about giving birth. What did you imagine it to be? Did it go as planned? Did you feel your world shift the first time you looked into your baby's eyes?

- Write about your fears. Many women experience anxiety, fears, worries, or stress after becoming mothers. Did you have any postpartum depression? Did a specific fear keep haunting you?

- Write about your belly. Write about it full and stretching with a child. Write about it loose with stretch marks after your baby was born. Write a love letter to your skin and the body that once housed your child.

- Write a letter to your child. Imagine that they can't open the letter for twenty years. What will you tell their future selves?

- Write about something your child loves. A toy, a book, a show, a person.

- Write about the difficulties of parenting. What frustrates you? What leaves you empty, angry? What makes you want to bang your head against a wall?

- Write about the joys of parenting. What surprised you about being a mother? What fills your heart with hope and unbounded love?

- Write an ode to a body part of yours. Write an ode to a body part of your baby's.

- Write about the less appealing stuff, the puke, the spit up, the tears, the poop, the pee, the blood.

Thanks for playing along! If you enjoyed these prompts or want to share your writing with me, please reach out. I'd love to hear from you.
jessicabateswriter@gmail.com

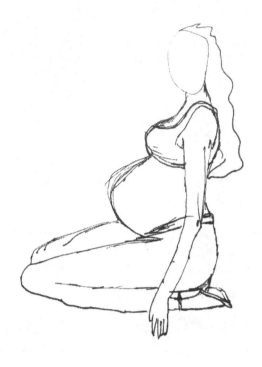

Progéniture
by Priscilla Charbonneau

36"x48" canvas, acrylic & burned copper

Priscilla reached out to photographer Cody Emberton after seeing our nursing portrait on social media. She asked if she could paint it, and we said yes! Thank you, Priscilla, for your beautiful work. *Progéniture* means "offspring" in French. Priscilla lives in Quebec.

There are some people I'd like to thank,
and so⋯

Thanks Cody Emberton for taking the photo on the cover. I will forever be stunned when I look at it. It makes me feel, and it puts me right back in that time. Thank you for responding to my whim of nude nursing portraits with such enthusiasm and speed! Otherwise I really might have lost the nerve. Ha!

Thanks Katie Vigos for starting Empowered Birth Project, and for posting the nude nursing portrait of you & your son that inspired the one on the cover. Thanks for pumping me up and giving me the balls — or rather, the tits — to be myself. Mothering is hard, and the community you cultivate at EBP helps empower mothers everywhere.

Thanks Priscilla Charbonneau for turning me into fine art. What a magical thing social media can be, when artists inspire other artists. Thanks for helping cultivate a serenity and sacredness around motherhood.

To all the mothers & fathers who have lost babies in utero or out — you are so strong. To the families struggling to conceive, stay strong. My heart is with you.

Thanks Leslie Hinson, for creating a place to share work and talk and connect. Thanks for listening to so many of these poems and giving such thoughtful feedback. I'm grateful for you & for our shared love of groups. Also thanks for all the good snacks and wine.

Thanks to the rest of my writer friends in The Paper State.

Thanks to my sisters, Chelsea and Maggie, for being my biggest supporters and best mirrors. I've learned so much about mothering and being a better human by watching you two teach kids & conquer life. I love you both so; cry emoji.

Thanks Mom & Dad. I really can't imagine better parents. Everyday as I parent I marvel at how cool, calm, and loving you both always were (and continue to be). Thanks for loving us hard and showing it and telling us again and again. Thanks for all the time you spent. I'm trying to live up to the example.

Thanks Mark. There wouldn't be a book or a baby without you. You're the best co-parent I could ask for, the yin to my yang. Let's make all the art until we die. Love you so.

Thanks Dax, for being a chill kid and letting me write poems. And thanks for making me a mother. I hope when you grow that this book doesn't embarrass you. All my love.

Thank you, dear reader, for getting this far. If you fancy, please consider leaving a review. They are essential to authors like me.

Made in the USA
Lexington, KY
24 October 2018